OK, Let's be Methodists

Mr Wesley preaching at Nottingham

OK,
Let's be Methodists

JOHN J. VINCENT

EPWORTH PRESS

7162 0397 9

First published 1984
by Epworth Press
Room 195, 1 Central Buildings
Westminster, London SW1

Typeset by Gloucester Typesetting Services
and printed in Great Britain by
Richard Clay Ltd (The Chaucer Press)
Bungay, Suffolk

All proceeds
from this book are donated to the
Urban Theology Unit and the
Sheffield Inner City Ecumenical Mission

To

the Members of

Grimesthorpe Methodist Church

('The Shop')

1984

*

Francis Butler	Richard Levitt
June Clarke	Anne Lewis
Elsie Greaves	Margaret Mackley
Florence Greaves	Ruth Thompson
John Greaves	Ethel Vincent
Florence Harrold	Grace Vincent

Contents

PROLOGUE

Is There Anything in Methodism?

The eighties . . .

The Church Union schemes flounder in Britain; there is endless delay in the USA.

Churches outside Methodism look into Wesley and find there are things they could use there.

Denominations everywhere rediscover their roots, use their histories to create new stories.

People in local churches ask, 'Are there methods we could be pursuing which would be better, more authentic?'

People in Methodism say, 'If we're going to have the label, shouldn't it mean something distinctive?'

People everywhere say, 'Is there anything any of you have got that might help us?'

The world says, 'We have problems, social, political, economic, do you have a method to tackle them?'

The world says, 'Do all churches have to be the same middle-class status institutions?'

The world says, 'Most of us are poor – is there anything for us?'

I say, There used to be things in Methodism that were answers to all these . . .

They could help us today,
change us,
bring us back to Jesus Christ
bring us back to his faith
his movement
his mission
his life-style
his community

So, I say, 'OK, let's be Methodists.' Or at least, 'Let's give it a whirl, and see what happens.'

ONE

Passion of the Heart

1. *The Spirit is upon me*

How do you 'get up and go?' How does a person who has become listless, or disappointed, or borne down with cares, obligations, routine become a person who is empowered, or hopeful, liberated, committed? How does someone for whom discipleship to Christ has become duty and obligation, become someone for whom it is joy and willing privilege? How does someone for whom membership of the church has become carrying out rules, customs and routines, become someone for whom it is an ever-expanding enterprise of new discovery? How does someone for whom the whole thing is like 'somebody else's show', landed on them, which they have to continue, become someone for whom it is 'My own Show', which they take up, and become a co-creator?

These are questions, it seems to me, which are illumined by Wesley's experience of 1738. He calls it moving 'from the religion of a servant to the religion of a son'. It was like changing from being a recipient of a system to becoming a dynamic part of that which creates systems.

The experience itself fitted into the existing 'salvation-scheme' as understood at the time. Under this scheme, especially as interpreted by the Moravians and Pietists, a person remained 'unsaved' until they had 'received' the forgiveness of sins. And the only way to be sure that your sins had been forgiven was either by having faith in the available mediation-system (Medieval Catholicism) or in the power of God (Luther) or in the providence of God (Calvin) or else – the option currently obsessing Wesley – in a distinct experience given by God. An evening weeping with the Moravian Peter Böhler on 26 April saw Wesley 'a poor, broken-hearted sinner, hungering after a better righteousness'. Then on 24 May, the catharsis Wesley was looking for occurred in Aldergate:

> I felt I did trust in Christ, Christ alone for salvation; and an assurance was given me that He had taken away *my* sins, even *mine*, and saved *me* from the law of sin and death.

Meantime, on 1 May 1738, the 'little society began, which afterwards met in Fetter Lane', mostly for mutual confession. In June 1738 Wesley went for three months to Germany to study the Moravian movement. From September 1738 until October 1739, Wesley was involved a great deal in getting the new societies in Bristol organized. In London a new Moravian pastor, Philip Molther, arrived and taught that people must remain in 'stillness' until God visited them. This John and Charles resisted, and violent divisions resulted, till Wesley opened his own headquarters at the Foundry on 11 November 1739, and in July 1740, about twenty of them finally left the Fetter Lane Society. These experiences seem to have given Wesley the courage to stand on his own feet, apart from the Moravians. But none of these gave Wesley the crucial 'get up and go'.

Albert Outler, I believe, has given us the decisive clue to Wesley's change from self-concern to mission, from anxiety about religious experience to compassion for those without religion. In his book *Evangelism in the Wesleyan Spirit* Outler writes:

> The sign-event of this remarkable conversion – not its cause, else we could duplicate his results simply by adopting his methods – was Wesley's embarrassed descent into field preaching on 2 April 1739. This was an even more decisive event for the Revival than Aldersgate – although, of course, without Aldersgate, this would scarcely have been possible. In any case, it was a shattering experience for the Oxford don who had hitherto cared so much more about 'delivering his own soul' than about the needs and dispositions of other people (p. 19).

The words which Wesley used in his Journal for 2 April are these:

> At four in the afternoon I submitted to be more vile and proclaimed in the highways the glad tidings of salvation, speaking from a little eminence in the ground adjoining to the city to about three thousand people. The scripture on which I spoke (is it possible any one should be ignorant that it is fulfilled in every true minister of Christ?) was, 'The Spirit of the Lord is upon me, because He hath anointed me to preach the gospel to the poor. He hath sent me to heal the broken-hearted; to preach deliverance to the captives, and recovery of sight to the blind; to set at liberty them that are bruised, to proclaim the acceptable year of the Lord.'

Outler goes on:

> Here his proclamation had finally passed over from highly self-conscious words to truly unselfconscious action. His passion for truth had been transformed into compassion for persons. This visible demonstration of his actual identification with them had stirred forlorn men to a real 'hearing of faith', and it was their hearing of faith that finally clinched Wesley's firm grasp upon his own faith. It was Wesley's belated success as an evangelist that finally made him into an assured believer (p. 20).

So it was that, in 1739–40, Wesley's societies in Bristol and London were joined by around 300 people in each place, and John had the delight of seeing his work appreciated and his societies being accepted and extended. From 1739, the Methodist Society welcomed everyone who wished to come. As Wesley puts it in *A Plain Account of the People Called Methodists* (1748):

> There is only one condition required in those who desire admission into this society – 'a desire to flee from the wrath to come, to be saved from their sins'.

The decisive break had taken place. Wesley was liberated. He had received his commission. The flood-gates were opened. He could get up and go. On 23 June 1739, he put it plainly in a letter to his brother Charles:

> I have both an ordinary call and an extraordinary call. My ordinary call is my ordination by the bishop. 'Take thou authority to preach the Word of God.' My extraordinary call is witnessed by the works that God doeth by my

ministry, which prove that He is of a Truth in the exercise of my office.

2. *The dead-end of distinctive doctrines*

Much labour has been expended on the question of the 'distinctive doctrines' of Methodism. Twenty years ago, the question was newly pushed to the fore by the proposed Service of Reconciliation, designed to bring the Anglican and Methodist Churches into a new united church, a proposal in fact approved by Methodism in 1967 and finally rejected by the Church of England in 1969. This Service of Reconciliation included the following:

> We Methodists, believing that within the One, Holy Catholic and Apostolic Church our communion was brought into being by the Holy Spirit to be a witness
> 1. to the universal grace of God,
> 2. to the gift of assurance by the Holy Spirit, and
> 3. to the power of the Holy Spirit to make us perfect perfect in love,
>
> desire to share with our brethren of the Church of England this our calling; and to enter into the spiritual heritage and continuity of commission which they treasure (*Report of the Conversations between the Church of England and the Methodist Church*, p. 38).

Other churches as well as Methodists were therefore compelled to consider these 'distinctive doctrines'. In 1965, I wrote a book called *Christ and Methodism* in which I considered the problems of each of them in some detail. While we have in fact heard much less about these 'distinctive doctrines' in more recent years, it is worth restating why I still think the discussion to be a 'dead-end'.

1. *Universality*. All churches now proclaim the universality of the gospel, including most Calvinistic ones, so that our 'emphasis' in this direction is no longer either significant or necessary. Today, it is not Universality, whether all may be saved or not, but Universalism, whether all are saved whether they know it or not, which divides people.

2. *Assurance*. The gift of assurance seems to have been at the heart of Wesley's experience of 24 May 1738. However, A. Skevington Wood and others have argued that this was Wesley's 'Conversion' experience. In fact, I prefer to speak of several 'conversions' in a person's life; 'assurance' could clearly be one such experience. But the idea of assurance as a particular gift, or as a particular 'witness' of a whole denomination, is really dependent on people actually having the experience. Assurance was perhaps a psychological need in Wesley's day, and quite often occurs in religious revivals. But it is largely absent today in any form remotely like that described by Wesley.

3. *Perfection*. Wesley's doctrine of Perfection was based on experiences of people in his day who claimed that God had given them the gift of 'Entire Sanctification', 'Holiness' or 'Perfection'. It is again a doubtful starter as a contemporary Methodist contribution. The experience and even the expectation of it are absent in most of Methodism today.

Justification by faith is usually linked with Universalism, Assurance, and Perfection as a special Methodist doctrine, but it has never been asserted that this was distinctive to Methodism.

The virtual disappearance of the Methodist 'distinctive doctrines' has left contemporary Methodists wondering what it is that we have to 'witness' to. Our doctrines are not, after all, so distinctive – and at the points where they are distinctive, they are no longer proper descriptions of our experience, so we cannot claim to 'possess' them. Whether we could ever have 'passed on' religious experiences to others was always an unmentioned problem. But now that we obviously do not even possess the experiences, we are apparently left without anything distinctive.

Or are we? Does not the dead-end to which the claims of distinctive doctrines have led us, in fact now leave us free to open up the story again, in a more constructive way?

It is my belief that it has.

3. Positively: contemporary questions

There are three things that, it seems to me, we can work on positively. Each one partly goes back to John Wesley's basic assumptions behind the doctrines.

1. *Religion of the heart.* The basis of all the experiential doctrines is the assumption that people can know God, experience God, become passionate lovers of God. It is the assumption that 'true religion' must be 'the religion of the warmed heart'.

> What we have felt and seen
> with confidence we tell
> And publish to the sons of men
> the signs infallible.

The origin of this emphasis lay in the presuppositions of Wesley's day – that a personal God would naturally make himself known to persons in a personal way – that is, in a 'spiritual' way, 'heart speaking to heart'. The result was that the Christian disciple could function on the basis of 'experiences' in which the 'heart was strangely warmed'.

The contemporary Methodist therefore has to know: What passions motivate disciples now? How do people today in fact become passionate disciples of the Way and passionate servants of Christ? How do individuals find themselves able to move from incapacity to liberation? What is the religion that people have 'in their hearts' that moves them now?

It is this question to which I shall turn in a moment. It is a matter of getting somehow some kind of 'get up and go'.

2. *Religion of divine activity.* Heart religion, however, is never to be self-induced. It is the result of the specific activities of God in the soul.

All the great doctrines, justification, assurance and sanctification, were part of Wesley's answer to the question, 'What does God do with people?'

1. How does God make people Christians? By justifying them, by giving them salvation, by faith alone.
2. But how can I know I am saved? By assurance, an inward conviction given by God.
3. But how shall I see the Lord? By holiness, by perfection, obedience, discipline and love.
4. But how can I know I am holy? Only by the revelation of God, giving me a distinct further blessing.

Thus, all the 'doctrines' are merely the *result* of God's activity. They attempt to explain specific actions of God in the soul. A Christian is a man 'born again' from above, by 'divine visitation', at every point.

The contemporary Methodist therefore has to know: What is God doing now? In what ways in our time does the divine activity present itself? What are the actions of God in the contemporary world? How does God manifest himself to individuals, to people, in the world? What are the dominant ways in which people describe their 'way' as Christians today?

This question will concern us throughout this book. The basic assumption of many contemporary Christians and theologians is that God works in the individual and personal area of human self-consciousness *as part of* the divine activities within humanity and history as a whole. So that we need to know 'What God does in the world', and 'What God does in history' – which is what we turn to in chapters 2 and 3.

3. *Experiential pragmatism.* John Wesley's theology is therefore a theology of pragmatism – theology 'making the best of it', in the light of what people are actually experiencing, and what God is actually doing. The value of experience means the elevation of pragmatism. As Wesley always insisted, doctrine and ecclesiology were being forced along by the work of the Holy Ghost active among his people. What people experience is actually what God is doing with them.

The contemporary Methodist therefore has to know: What theology is being created on the basis of reality now? What is the witness and testimony of disciples? What is the experience of individuals and communities? If an empirical, pragmatist, opportunist spirit is basic to Methodism, we now need to apply this to people's discipleship today, as they actually experience it.

This question is essentially the question about what makes a person a disciple, and what makes a community of people into a church. These are the themes of chapters 3 and 4. When we have seen again what actually happened in

Wesley's times, and what is happening now, and what might happen in the future, we will know what there is to 'experience'.

4. *Get up and go*

I believe that the originating experience of John Wesley is best described in terms of two biblical notions – those of call and messianic consciousness.

1. *Call.* Men and women get 'called' in the Bible in a variety of different ways. Yet there are certain characteristics of Calls which can be found in all the call stories, whether in the Old or the New Testament. (i) Persons called are usually called out of something preoccupying them, into something completely different. Thus Wesley is called from inward soul-searching to mission to the poor. (ii) Persons called do not know what precisely they are called to, but have to learn to 'follow'. Thus Wesley regarded himself as a servant being led 'where he knew not'. (iii) Persons called set aside everything else to fulfil what they feel they are called to. Thus Wesley set aside his Oxford fellowship, and retained his status as a Church of England minister as it served his new calling to a ministry where 'the world is my parish'. (iv) Persons with a call have to face criticism and ridicule from others. Thus Wesley had to insist more and more on the 'extra-ordinary ministry' he found himself led to. (v) Persons called invariably develop a strong inward conviction or consciousness of their own status as someone distinctly 'sent'. This is clear in all Wesley's writings – and produces what I call a 'messianic consciousness'.

2. *Messianic consciousness.* This term is used to describe the personal consciousness which is the originating force within

a person, empowering or enabling him or her to pursue a God-given call. Scholars of the New Testament debate how far we may speak of a 'messianic self-consciousness' in Jesus – or, even more, how far we may know anything about it. Certainly, Jesus speaks of having been 'sent', of having a 'cup of destiny to fulfil' of being 'straightened' till he has done what he has to do, of there being a 'time', a *kairos*, which legitimates and necessitates his work. Jesus talks of some things as 'possible', and some as not possible. The 'messianic self-consciousness' is a way of seeking to say something about the inner awareness which makes all this possible. Very similar language is used by Paul in his talk of his having an apostolic task, of his having this task 'laid upon him', of his being 'sent'.

John Wesley, similarly, spoke of his work as 'apostolic'. He acted on the assumption that the gospel gave him all the imperatives he needed, and it was his business to get on and carry them out. Such was, indeed, the calling, in Wesley's view, of every Christian. Yet he acted on it – and unquestionably felt the divine compulsion to do so. He did not hesitate to say that the Spirit was upon him. So, on Monday, 2 April 1739, his first open-air sermon was on the text: 'The Spirit of the Lord is upon me, because he has anointed me to preach the Gospel to the poor' – explicitly applying the text both to Jesus and to himself. And he comments: 'Is it possible any one should be ignorant, that it is fulfilled in every true Minister of Christ?'

One mark of a genuine messianic-consciousness is that it is necessitated by the ridicule, criticism and questioning of others. No one requires a messianic-consciousness to perform actions for which there is outside, constitutional, or authoritative legitimation. Jesus, Paul and Wesley each lacked this kind of outside authorization, and therefore had to insist that they did what they did basically on the strength of inner conviction of its rectitude – or, even more, basic inner conviction that they were 'anointed' and this legitimized, by God.

I have used the term 'messianic', because this is biblically correct. The word 'messiah' simply means 'anointed'. When Jesus is proclaimed as being 'the Messiah', the Christ, what is meant is that he has been uniquely anointed by God as the one who is to herald and make possible God's kingdom. This does not mean that others also cannot be 'messianic'. Indeed, on the contrary, it means that, now, God's anointing, God's spirit-giving, God's empowering, is available to people in a wholly new and more extensive way, like the Spirit poured on to 'all flesh' in Acts 2.23.

Thus, the Messianic consciousness is available to all.

John Wesley does not seem to have made anything much of his personal sense of being called, or of having a consciousness that he was entitled to do what he did. He would say that every Christian is called to do what he did, and thus would be empowered to carry it out. His consciousness is pedestrian, participatory and unexclusive. And precisely for this reason is he such a good model or inspiration for us.

One of the problems with any institution or denomination is that the functions of ministry have been regularized and organized to be performed by certain persons who are 'authorized' to carry them out. Wesley himself soon got into the business of such authorization. And it is essential that the authorizing function takes place, and that it should be carried out in as democratic a way as possible.

But what we need above all today is not more and more people authorized by others to do this or that. What we need is more and more people saying 'this thing I must do', 'it seems good to the Spirit and to us to do so-and-so', 'constraint is upon me – woe is me if I do not this piece of the gospel'. And precisely this is what Wesley saw himself faced with, and precisely this is what formed the first Methodism – as we shall see in the next chapter.

For us today, it simply and sufficiently means that nothing happens in the world or the church or the realm of the Spirit or the long history of humanity – until someone from whatever source or situation begins to say with passion, 'this one thing I must do'.

Passion of the heart is the base of all true Christianity. The story of Wesley shows how an inverted passion can lead to destruction, but how an extraverted passion can lead to salvation. The 'heart strangely warmed' is the beginning of all true conviction; what stirs it and keeps it warm is not simply 'an inward conviction' but also a heart set to love the Lord our God with all our heart and soul and mind and strength, and also to love our neighbour with that heart and soul and mind and strength with which we love ourselves.

This is the passion of the heart to which Wesley points us.

TWO

Rising of the Poor

1. *A movement of common people*

It is natural to assume that Wesley *was* Methodism; that he created, defined, controlled it. Certainly without him, without his very strong and distinctive style and conviction, there would be no Methodism as we know it. But it is quite clear that there was a strong religious movement that Wesley did not start. There was already a widespread popular movement arising, indeed functioning in several parts of the country. Not only was there a great readiness among the hearers for the kind of powerful faith and intimate societies that proliferated with Wesley, but the work was already springing up in certain parts of England around a surprising number of individual preachers, prior to and quite separate from Wesley.

The main centres of Wesley's work were London (from 1738), Bristol (from 1739) and Newcastle (from 1742). One reason for this is that other evangelists were already at work in other places. John Bennet developed a wide circuit of societies and preaching places in Lancashire, Cheshire and Derbyshire. Selina, Countess of Huntingdon, built a vast connection across the North of England, mainly and exceptionally for the upper classes! In the North, too, Thomas Lee created societies out of his work place, the worsted trade. John Haime worked in a similar way within the expeditionary army, as did John Nelson in the West Riding. These and many others, in varying degrees, created new Christian work out of a people who clearly everywhere were ready for it. Some of these made links with Wesley, or even joined him, with relief and enthusiasm. Others never connected with his movement. What is crucial and significant is that they were there both before Wesley and independently of him.

One important characteristic of Wesley's movement arises from the fact of this existing mass, popular awakening. The preachers and the members of his societies were, almost without exception, from the ordinary working people, from the bottom of society. A list of Bristol preachers in 1741 includes '2 hoopers, 2 weavers, 2 mastermariners, 2 braziers, a house carpenter, a serge maker, a cork cutter' ... and so on.

Not only were his preachers simple, working people, but Wesley 'sat at their feet'. They were often condemned as 'a few, raw, young, unlettered men' (*Journal*, 16 June 1755). But Wesley's sole criterion was whether a potential preacher had a spiritual power and a conviction to declare. He neither demanded education, nor offered it to his preachers. The 'travelling bookshop' in their saddle-bags was mainly religious biography. And he gave them enormous freedom to function as they were called. He trusted their call and learned from them. He believed God was at work and trusted him to continue it. Sometimes he was criticized for too easily giving a recommended person a licence to travel. But he was facilitating the work of God, not controlling it. Of course, control would in practice have been very difficult. He could not visit often and his only means of communication was the horse! But neither did he wish it.

Wesley received a great degree of acceptance and affection from the common people. He became ultimately more uncomfortable with the upper class, Oxford or London society, than with his Kingswood colliers. The massive awakening and response to his work was among such people. They affirmed the rightness of his work. Wesley might well have gained his decisive assurance, not from the Aldersgate Street 'heartwarming', but from seeing the New Testament church come alive among the common people. He then knew, assuredly, that he and his work were acceptable to God.

A recent unpublished essay by Bernard Hall on 'New Model Church' points out many of these elements and shows how, in fact, this artisan, grassroots, unordained, and untrained leadership was decisive for the whole of Wesley's lifetime and immediately afterwards. Indeed, Wesley's special places, London and Bristol, preserved an ordained ministry style – Charles came to London when John had to be away! – which was totally unique. Bernard Hall observes how the itinerant preachers who died before 1800 were rarely from London or Bristol (only 9) and even Wesley's Newcastle produced only 8, whereas 26 were from Yorkshire, 12 from adjacent counties, 18 were from Ireland, 11 from Cornwall, and 16 from elsewhere. The conclusion is plain: Bennet, Grimshaw, Darney and Nelson produced far more preachers than Wesley! Perhaps Sarah Crosby illustrates this most strongly. In London she was but a class leader. Moving to Derby, where there were no Methodists, she soon found a building and a congregation, and she became a preacher and leader.

Bernard Hall also sees the widespread popular religious movement in Wesley's time as a continuation of the Puritan tradition in the previous century which had been repressed by the law under the Restoration with the Act of Toleration of 1688.

2. *An alternative to revolution?*

The movement in which Wesley participated was thus a 'rising of the poor' in the sense that it was a movement of poor people, claiming for themselves a place within the religion of the time, which they had been otherwise denied, and creating for themselves societies and associations to support and extend their new-found consciousness.

But the movement was also a 'rising of the poor' in a more literal sense. The poor cried out from dire distress, and sought real change. In his sermon on 'National Sins and Miseries' in 1775, Wesley says:

> That the people suffer, none can deny . . . thousands of people in the west of England, throughout Cornwall in particular, in the north, and even in the midland counties, are totally unemployed . . . I have seen not a few of these wretched creatures . . . standing in the streets, with pale looks, hollow eyes, and meagre limbs; or creeping up and down like walking shadows. I have known families, who a few years ago lived in an easy, genteel manner, reduced to just as much raiment as they had on, and as much food as they could gather in the field. To this one or other of them repaired once a day, to pick up the turnips which the cattle had left; which they boiled, if they could get a few sticks, or, otherwise, ate them raw (*Works*, vii, p. 402).

It was this situation that produced a 'rising of the poor' for which the early Methodist societies provided a salutary place for at least a new self-consciousness and the exercise of charity.

Whether early Methodism provided anything more has been hotly debated. Elie Halevy argued that Methodism not only saved England from a French revolution, but also diverted into religious channels energies that could have secured social, economic and political reform. The argument has been hotly debated. Recently, Bernard Semmel, in *The Methodist Revolution* argues that Methodism was in fact the British form of the Democratic Revolution. He says:

> I am persuaded by historians who see the period between 1760 and 1815 as an '*Age of the Democratic Revolution*' in the West, a time when the traditional, hierarchical society which had characterized Europe for many centuries was eroding and a recognizable modern society was taking its place. This was a time when the entire Atlantic world, moved by the desire for greater personal autonomy and roused by the slogans of liberty and equality, rose to overturn the privileged, governing classes, bringing the long-suppressed, inarticulate lower classes, onto the stage of events (p. 7).

Thus, Methodism may have helped to block a violent English counterpart to the French Revolution by pre-empting the critical appeal and objective of that Revolution, and providing a counter to revolutionary violence.

The 'rising of the poor', then, at least in Wesley's day, and in the century which followed, did not produce the necessary social and economic reforms. Indeed, Methodism soon developed a more 'establishment' face, in line with Wesley's own innate Toryism. Thus, it would be possible for our Sheffield radical poet, Ebenezer Elliott, to write in his 'Open-Air Sermon' of 1833:

Ask ye if I, of Wesley's followers one,
Adjure the house where Wesleyans bend the knee?
I do – because the *Spirit* thence is gone;
And truth, and faith, and grace, are not, with me,
The Hundred Popes of England's Jesuitry.
What are the *deeds* of men called Christian, now?
They roll themselves in dust before the great;
Wherever Mammon builds a shrine, they bow,
And would nail Jesus to their cross of hate,
Should he again appear in *mean* estate . . .
Pious they are, cool, circumspect, severe;
And while they feel for woes beyond the wave,
They laud the tyrants who starve millions here:
The famish'd Briton *must* be fool or knave,
But wrongs are precious in a foreign slave.
Their Bibles for the heathen load our fleets;
Lo! gloating eastward, they inquire, 'What news?'
'We die,' we answer, 'foodless, in the streets,'
And what reply your men of Gospel-views?
Oh, 'they are sending bacon to the Jews!'
Their lofty souls have telescopic eyes,
Which see the smallest speck of distant pain,
While, at their feet, a world of agonies,
Unseen, unheard, unheeded, writhes in vain.

Thus did Wesley's successors desert the poor. And the poor had to look elsewhere for their revolution. The question that fascinates me, however, is whether there is not a revolution attainable by incarnation. Wesley became incarnate among the poor, the labouring artisans, the powerless people. He completely believed in their worth, so that his highest praise was to say that someone was like one of the

Kingswood colliers. 'O that our London brethren would come to school at Kingswood,' he once wrote. The poor grew to love him, too. He fitted into their world. So much was this true that he no longer felt at ease among the Oxford and London upper classes where he began.

His style of living reflected his real incarnation into the world of working people. He kept a very simple 'cell' in London, Bristol and Newcastle. When elsewhere, he stayed with his preachers. He lived on £28 a year and gave away the rest to the poor. He urged and practised a diligent frugality. He saw to it that all the giving of his people went to the poor. Only in later Methodism was most of it deflected into buildings and ministerial salaries, with only a token 'Poor Fund' left at an infrequent sacrament. So fundamental was his rooting among the poor that several of his successors as President, after his death, were from the artisan, or even less skilled groups.

In a leaflet addressed to his fellow clergy, Wesley says: 'The rich, the honorable, the great, we are thoroughly willing to leave to you. Only let us alone with the poor, the vulgar, the base, the outcasts of men.' And to George II he declared: 'We are inconsiderable people, a people scattered afield and trodden underfoot. Silver and gold have we none.'

Wesley had joined a movement of the common people, and that is the first stage of a true revolution. Only when we are there can we ask, What does 'mission alongside the poor' mean?

3. *Mission alongside the poor*

The situation facing Britain in the eighties and probably the nineties is not propitious. Unemployment persists at 4 to 6 million, the figure dependent on who you include in the number. The inner city and other urban and rural deprived areas continue to receive less and less of the attention of the rest of the nation. The divisions widen between rich and poor, qualified and unqualified, healthy and sick, middle class and non-working class, those in the South East and those in the North.

In this situation the churches will naturally expand their traditional 'ambulance' roles. We probably will be pressed almost beyond endurance, simply to try to provide adequate healing, helping and supporting ministries. The Methodist Church has long been engaged in this.

In 1983, British Methodism commenced a new programme of 'Mission Alongside the Poor'. We are busy raising a million pounds for it. That will help. But we need to move beyond it. 'Mission Alongside the Poor' thrusts the Christian church into the forefront of the contemporary political implications and possibilities of our own reports and policies.

1. We are called to *economic and social discipleship*. The church has for generations taken sides in the division between rich and poor in Britain. It has taken sides and remained faithful to its main base in recent decades – the middle class. Now the church is pledging itself to stand alongside the poor. We shall not remain the same if we do this. We shall become different people. The values, the culture, the life-styles of the poor will become influential for us. This is a political act of discipleship. It means that our traditional assumptions, presuppositions, attitudes and opinions have to be questioned – not because we change our origins (which we cannot), but because we now stand beside different kinds of people.

This means that we are committed to taking sides in the economic battles for survival which divide Britain today. We have to become alert to new voices – the voices of the poor, the deprived, the immigrant, the people of other faiths and life-styles. I believe that this is where Methodist Christians at least naturally belong. But it may mean refusing promotion, rejecting upward mobility, avoiding professional advance, and taking downward journeys. Many people, I believe, will respond to this. Many people will come and join us because of it. Three times a year, at the Urban Theology Unit, we have conferences on 'Vocation in the Eighties' for people in their twenties and thirties, which bear out this fact. We are already seeing the beginnings of an economic journey downwards of Christian people to become incarnate among the poor and find ways to mission alongside them.

Christian people today – and we Methodists also – are called to carry out a new analysis of the actual situation in our society which causes the situation facing the poor. And then to look at the implications of that for our understanding of contemporary political options – whether capitalist or socialist.

2. We are called to *political discipleship*. Britain at present has no political party which adequately represents the poor. The Conservative Party is revealed as the party of division, privilege and social injustice. The Labour Party remains the party of the working class – that is, those with jobs, those who can join Trades Unions. The Social Democratic Party and the Liberal Party care for the managers, and probably many Methodists! Who cares for the poor?

We are in a situation in which we as a church, by missioning alongside the poor, have to become their political allies

– not to speak for them, but to speak *with* them. At present the 4 to 6 million unemployed people in Britain are disenfranchized. We must work to create new political alliances and organizations to speak with the poor, so that those who have no voice at present may obtain one. This will be a hard road. But our commitment to the poor will demand it of us.

Hence, we need, with others, to develop political alliances which will make it possible for the voice of the poor to be heard. Labour, SDP, Liberal and Conservative cannot speak for the poor. Neither can we *yet*, but we could *learn* from the poor. Mission *alongside* the poor means allowing God's mission through the poor to find allies. The church must be prepared to confront 'the powers that be' in industry, government, and even trades unions. We must assist a nationwide 'Opposition Party' to include the poor.

3. We are called to *entrepreneurial discipleship*. The programme of 'Mission Alongside the Poor' can easily be seen as a measure simply to alleviate the most cruel implications of current government policies, simply as a 'bandaid' which does not alter fundamental realities. The original Notice of Motion which started all this, which I proposed at the Conference of 1980, asked that we also work at the *causes* of inequality. So we must see out our modest efforts within our church as a way to get going things which can somehow survive in a political climate which is opposed to them.

In the Sheffield Inner City Ecumenical Mission, we employ a hundred people on a Manpower Services Scheme – but 80–90% of them will go back on to unemployment. So our main aim now is to try to get co-operative work-sharing and skill-sharing going, during their year on an MSC Scheme, which will issue in full or part time work for them at the end of it. We need to become entrepreneurs amongst those who have often lost the will or ability to create the future they or we need.

Thus, we need to see our activities in Mission Alongside the Poor as 'political parables'. They are not designed only to help people who suffer injustice. They are intended to be models, examples, parables of the ways in which society in general can deal in a larger way with these problems. So we must become political campaigners on the basis of our work.

4. *A Methodism of the poor?*

In places, there is a new mood in Methodism today. There is a new recovery of confidence. There are many large churches and excellent congregations. There are many missions and circuits which are really tackling the problems and doing a wonderful job.

But the question is, Where is 'strength' from the Christian point of view? The Christian gospel, and the work of Jesus, are all about the significance of what is 'down'. The whole gospel is about 'life at the bottom'. It is only when you are down that the gospel happens.

What does this mean for Methodism? Does it not mean that we have got to reverse our policies? At present, we are far away from participating in any 'rising of the poor', either in terms of assisting the poor to have a gospel and a gospel community within their own neighbourhoods, life-styles and cultures, or in terms of being alongside them in their claim for betterments. Indeed, the opposite is the case.

Far from being good news for the poor, we are bad news for the poor. Far from standing beside them in their rising up, we continue to keep them down. We have been closing down little churches, deserting people at the bottom, removing surviving recalcitrant local leaders, all my ministry. We close down between 100 and 125 chapels every year. In every case, we pull out of some area where we 'could not do well'. Often such areas are inner-city areas, rural areas, small down-town areas, small towns – all the places where the little old Methodist Chapel, Primitive, United or Wesleyan, used to be, one on each street corner.

We have systematically pulled out of such places and concentrated on the places where we could 'do well'. Where we cannot 'do well', we pack up our bags and go. And the places we leave are the places where working-class Methodism used to be – Cardiff, Swansea, Cymru, London SE and the predominantly industrial Northern districts of Liverpool, Manchester, Newcastle, Tees-side and Yorkshire.

What has happened is simply that the 'successful' style of Methodism only works where 'big' things and 'big' people can function. We have obliterated more and more elements of 'the bottom'. We have become part of the oppression of the poor.

So, we have to ask, can Methodism urgently now before it is too late concentrate its attention on the small places at the bottom where we still have some witness, and find new ways in which such groups can survive? Can we not also see this as a new way to develop in the future, doing as John Wesley did, getting small groups of people in any place to create a society, not necessarily in a building, to be people of Christ as a small community within a small neighbourhood?

Admittedly, we continue to attract some young people. But are these young people being brought into a full blooded discipleship understanding of vocation, careers, places to live, styles of life, and basic assumptions? Or are they merely being brought into culture-affirming *status quo* Christianity? Four conferences I took in 1983 with four University Methodist Societies in various places make me wonder.

And there is real life still among many of our little chapels among the poor. It is hard going, but often there is life at the bottom. In many churches, the young people have got a completely different ethos, a life and community of their own. Will Methodism be able to let them develop into self-conscious Christian communities? Or will we lose them because we expect them to fit into the established ways of the adult church? Again the genius of John Wesley can help us. He allowed and encouraged groups of people with particular life-styles to come together and create Christian communities – societies, he called them – and provide their own support.

So, we are 'down but not out'. But equally, 'life' is at the bottom, and we need to start building again around the life at the bottom, and not think that we can use the situation merely to prop up the top-heavy, large, expensive church models that Methodism is being confined to. I believe this is the hope for the future. But we will only do this if we are prepared to liberate ourselves from the idea that in order to have a church, you must have large numbers, big buildings.

What we have experienced within the Sheffield Inner City Ecumenical Mission now probably needs to be carried further as an alternative strategy for authentic Methodism. This means that we rediscover the gospel, and we rediscover the Lord, in at least three ways:

1. We reflect his *journey downwards*. As he constantly sought out new places and people where he had to be and become incarnate again, so we in the inner city constantly seek new

places where we must journey downwards to find places where incarnation is demanded.

2. We reflect his *Blessed are the poor*. This Jesus meant for his disciples. They are those who had become poor for the kingdom. Precisely this life-style of reversals is our experience and our joy.

3. We reflect his *undistinguishing regard*. Jesus welcomed all. But especially he welcomed bottom people, outsiders, foreigners, the unexpected. So we seek out those outside the conventional Christian folds, and encourage new forms of disciple groups or para-church arising around and for them.

THREE

Radical Discipleship

1. *Having things in common*

John Wesley believed that the events of the 1740s were bringing about a recall of New Testament Christianity. One significant aspect of this primitive Christianity, to which Wesley felt particularly attracted, was that of the community of goods.

There seems to have been two origins of this: first, a sense of call to re-establish the earliest Christianity in all its aspects; and second, a sense of the needs of those who suffered most from economic injustice. There was never any question that the economic needs of the poor, who belonged to the societies, had to be met. The entry in Wesley's Journal for Thursday 7 May 1741 dramatically indicates this:

> I reminded the United Society, that many of our brethren and sisters had not needful food; many were destitute of convenient clothing; many were out of business, and that without their own fault; and many sick and ready to perish: that I had done what in me lay to feed the hungry, to clothe the naked, to employ the poor, and to visit the sick; but was not, alone, sufficient for these things; and therefore desired all whose hearts were as my heart:

1. To bring what clothes each could spare, to be distributed among those that wanted most.

2. To give weekly a penny, or what they could afford, for the relief of the poor and sick.

My design, I told them, is to employ, for the present, all the women who are out of business and desire it, in knitting.

To these we will first give the common price for what work they do; and then add, according as they need.

Twelve persons are appointed to inspect these, and to visit and provide things needful for the sick.

Each of these is to visit all the sick within their district, every other day: and to meet on Tuesday evening, to give an account of what they have done, and consult what can be done farther.

The sharing of material goods – or sharing the lack of them – was thus an obvious implication of the life of a normal Christian community.

Wesley carried this further in his plans to create 'a community of goods', which was discussed in the following years. In a conversation with John Wesley, contained in the Diary of a Mr Viney, it is recorded for Wednesday 22 February 1744:

He (Wesley) told me of an intention he and some few have of beginning a Community of goods, but on a plan which I told him I doubted could not succeed. Tis this: each is to bring what cash they have and put it together. If anyone shall owe debts, they are first to be paid. Then each abiding in their dwellings and following their Business as they do now, are to bring weekly, what they earn and put it into the common box, out of which they are again to receive weekly, as much as is thought necessary to maintain their Families, without reflecting whether they put much or little into Ye Box (*Wesley Historical Society Proceedings*, Vol. XIV, pp. 29–30).

Thomas Madron, in an article on 'Some Aspects of Wesley's Economic Thought Revisited', argues that the opposition to this ideal being practically implemented was so strong that Wesley had to relent after 1744. His rules of 'gain, save and give all you can' constitute a compromise. As late as 1760 a pamphlet sought to dissuade 'all serious and well-disposed Methodists from their notion of the Community of Christian Men's Goods'. The conviction that Methodism stood for such a notion persisted so strongly that Thomas Coke, after the death of Wesley, was forced to issue an official denial (*Methodist History*, Vol. IV, October 1965, pp. 34–45).

But clearly Wesley's view of property and his interest in commonality led to a strong co-operative spirit in Methodism. He established a 'lending stock', a sort of credit union, to enable people to borrow without interest, and a 'Strangers' Friend Society' in London in 1785 for 'the relief, not of our society, but for the poor, sick, friendless strangers'. While Wesley said, 'Gain all you can, save all you can, and give all you can', in fact, his constant emphasis was upon giving away. To the rich man he cries, 'Be ye ready to distribute to every one, according to his necessity' (Sermon XXVIII, *Works*, Vol. VI, p. 376). Wesley felt 'the highest concept of economic organization' to be that of 'primitive communism', the kind of organization which he thought obtained among the earliest Christians. The Rules for the Select

Societies written by the first Conference of 1744 included: Every member, till we have all things in common, will bring once a week, *bona fide*, all he can toward a common stock.

Richard Viney says the idea resembled the socialist ideal, 'from each according to his ability, to each according to his need'. Thus, though Wesley's early hopes were not fulfilled, he consistently denied the duty of 'getting a good estate'. He also denied the common contemporary view that property was held as some sacred inviolable right. Rather, the right to property is bound to its proper use. Thus, Wesley rejected what has been called the 'Protestant ethic'. He opposed the enclosure movement, and the monopolization of the farms (*Letters*, Vol. V, p. 352). He advocated a new distribution of land, and urged 'letting no farms of above a hundred pounds a year' (*Letters*, Vol. V, p. 354).

2. *The problem of affluence*

Thus, though Wesley's hopes for a primitive communism were not fulfilled, he remained a severe critic of wealth. The affluence of the rich and privileged was a constant concern to him. Indeed, in some 'thoughts upon Methodism' written towards the end of his life – in 1787 – Wesley wrote:

> I fear, whenever riches have increased (exceeding few are the exceptions), the essence of religion, the mind that was in Christ, has decreased in the same proportion. Therefore I do not see how it is possible in the nature of things, for any revival of true religion to continue long. For religion must necessarily produce both industry and frugality; and these cannot but produce riches. But as riches increase, so

will pride, anger, and love of the world in all its branches (*Arminian Magazine*, 10 (1787), p. 156).

Wesley's declaration is striking, that an increase in riches (meaning *personal* riches) leads to a decrease in 'the mind that was in Christ', in the same proportion. But his assumption that an increase in religion will lead to industry, frugality, and therefore riches could be questioned, even if history has proved him right. Piety does not have to lead to personal wealth. Perhaps piety leads to wealth in the system of personal religion Wesley developed. People were formed into societies the better to seek their own and the other members' *personal* sanctification. So riches acquired by such personally pietistic life-style would easily be seen as their own.

Thus, I must conclude that Wesley did not push far enough, or see as crucial enough, the 'having all things in common' in which case the riches would never be *theirs*, but rather riches shared *in community*. Then if he were to have pushed that farther still into a critical analysis of the whole wealth of the country, and pushed his people to see their battles on the wider political front as a crucial part of their 'sanctification', then religion could not lead to greater personal riches. Albert Finney perhaps saw this when he added to Wesley's 'Gain all you can, save all you can, give all you can' the anti-capitalist virtue, 'Sell as *cheap* as you can.' And Methodism has been conspicuously a social escalator in its two centuries so far.

Wesley and the early Methodist preachers demonstrate that piety does not necessarily lead to affluence. Indeed, on the contrary, poverty leads to self-discipline and self-denial. In the Holy Club at Oxford (1725–30), Wesley found that he could live on £28 per year, a frugality which he continued throughout his life. The Holy Club practised confession, penance and mortification, as well as fasts on Wednesdays and Fridays till 3 p.m. At the same time, they maintained a school for needy children, and took food, clothes and medicine for the poor in St Thomas's Workhouse and in the city. The term 'Methodist' was first flung at them in derision as those whose life-style followed such a rigorous 'method'. Wesley welcomed the term, and later said: 'A Methodist is one who lives according to the Method laid down in the Bible.'

Again, Wesley and his preachers discovered that an apostolic ministry was meaningless and impossible unless it was conducted by those who put themselves alongside those to whom they were ministering. Wesley's statement that he and the other preachers 'diet with the poor, on the same food, and at the same table' meant that he and they lived in London at 'The Poor House', with nine widows, one blind woman, two poor children, and two upper servants – 'a comfortable earnest of our eating bread together in our Father's Kingdom'. Francis Asbury took up the same note in his comments to the early American Methodist preachers: 'We must suffer *with* if we labour *for* the poor.' The first Methodist circuit riders took Asbury's advice literally, and sheltered in dirty cabins, slept in comfortless beds, and shared the poverty of the poor.

The problem of affluence can be dealt with in two ways. First, you may be generous with your affluence. By and large, we have assumed this is to be the only way. But there is a second way. You can renounce your affluence, or greatly reduce it. This latter, it seems to me, is the message we now need to hear.

Recently, I have come to preaching these 'alternative

journeys' around the universities. The response has become slowly more welcoming! I tell them that the call of Christ means:

1. *A journey backwards.* Jesus began his ministry with a call for a Jubilee, a cancellation of debts and injustices by 'going back' to a state of freedom and authenticity.

2. *A journey sideways.* Jesus invited people to leave the Israel of the day and form an 'alternative community', represented first in the Twelve, and then in the earliest church.

3. *A journey downwards.* Jesus took their money and livelihoods off the Twelve, and then proclaimed: 'Happy are you poor'.

I am often asked: 'But does God not love the affluent?'

There are several answers. (1) Jesus welcomed the rich and used them when they could serve him and the kingdom. (2) Jesus warned the rich man that 'it is easier for a camel to go through a needle's eye than for a rich man to get into the kingdom of God'. (3) Jesus also expected much more from the rich than from the poor. 'Much is expected from those to whom much is given.'

The 'alternative journey' brings its own rewards. But it has to be taken seriously before it takes us joyfully! So, Wesley wrote to a Miss March on 7 February 1776:

> Creep in among these (the poor) in spite of dirt and an hundred disgusting circumstances, and thus put off the gentlewoman. Do not confine your conversation to genteel and elegant people. I should like this as well as you do; but I cannot discover a precedent for it in the life of our Lord or any of His Apostles. My dear friend, let us walk as He walked.

3. The new obedience – 1

So, we need to begin to draw up the lines of a new radical discipleship, fitted for our age, as Wesley's was for his.

In every case, we must do what Wesley did – look at the contemporary situation, look at the gospel, and look for new obediences. Radical discipleship is never a matter of searching out strange new implications of the gospel – it is always a matter of bringing together situation, gospel, and opportunity.

So, we seek a four-fold discovery. We seek a discovery of what is really happening in the world and to people. We seek a new discovery of the Man of Nazareth. We look to Wesley to see if he can help. And we seek a new obedience of disciples round Jesus today.

Our 'mission in the eighties' thus emerges – in six areas at least. All are 'signposts' to point disciples to search for contemporary implications; three in the area of corporate and national life, three in the areas of personal life and attitudes.

1. *Consumerism.* Unending pressure to buy, to spend, to replace a simpler possession with a more complex and more expensive one, is a fundamental part of how Western society functions. Every young child is taught it, in every area of its experience – home, school, peers, social life. This drive is fed by advertising, but goes deeper into the consciousness than that.

The preaching of Jesus is just in a different place altogether. The basis of satisfaction is to 'have all and follow'. Riches prevent you getting into the kingdom. In practice, following Jesus and holding on to possessions are totally incompatible.

John Wesley quite simply practised what his Master

taught. His style, and that which he urged on all his people, was one of asceticism.

> I do not mean avoid gluttony only: an honest mother would condemn these. But there is a regular, reputable kind of sensuality, an elegant epicurism which does not immediately disorder the stomach nor impair the understanding yet it cannot be maintained without considerable expense. Cut off all this expense. Despise delicacy and variety and be content with what plain nature requires (*Journal*, 7 May 1741).

The new obedience for today must begin in *asceticism*. The only way whereby we can meet the problems of consumerism, of over-consumption, of unnecessary luxury, is by developing a wholly alternative scale of value which is able to dismiss such things.

Asceticism may sound negative. But asceticism is basically the setting on one side of unimportant things, so that worthwhile things can be pursued. We must discover how to liberate ourselves from the consciousness upon which consumerism feeds. A clear and vigorous asceticism could be the first nail into its coffin.

2. *Economic inequality*. There is a growing recognition of increasing poverty and a steadily widening gap between rich and poor in Britain today. Research done for the London Weekend Television series, *Breadline Britain*, shown in September 1983, revealed that, by a standard arrived at by the judgment of the large number interviewed, 7·5 million people in Britain today are poor. 1 in 7 are dependent on Supplementary Benefit, 1 in 9 lack some essential item of clothing, and 1 in 18 cannot afford to heat the living areas of their homes. No less than 71% of those judged poor

by the programme live in the North and Midlands, 10% in London and 20% in the rest of the South.

And the converse of all this is also starkly true. In 1981, the Home Missions Division and the Urban Theology Unit produced a report, *Two Nations, One Gospel?* in which this contrast was shown visibly and in detail. Today, with galloping cuts in the Welfare State, the situation is infinitely worse.

Jesus was clearly acutely aware of the extreme inequality of his society. He declared riches to be totally incompatible with the kingdom, he demanded that would-be disciples get rid of them – Zaccheus, rich young ruler – and he lived alongside the poor.

Wesley's superb contribution was to move from one side of the divide to the other. As we have seen, he would have loved to spend time with the rich, but could see no precedent for it in the life of Jesus, and so did not. From 1751, when his Oxford fellowship ceased, he lived continually on his £28 a year, although his income rose from £30 to £120. The rest was given to the poor. He ensured that he only carried £8 over from one year to the next. And he died with his £8 – sufficient for a funeral.

In a grossly divided society such as we live in today, the only contribution of any value that Christians can make is to move from one side of the divide to the other.

The New Obedience thus is that alternative Christians will find a way to leap the divide. Then, and only then, will they have any word about inequality.

Can this be the distinctiveness for Methodists today? In the past they stood out on issues of action and life-style, such as alcohol; could we demonstrate a similarly clear example on inequality today?

3. *Worklessness.* Worklessness is part of the fabric of society in the 1980s. We search for solutions, superficial or radical. We growingly accept it and are forced to turn to new ways of deploying time and energy, and acquiring self-respect, either for bits of profit or leisure. Fewer and fewer people are going to be needed to keep the technological and industrial societies going, and more and more people are going to be left high and dry. The 'alternative society' is already in our midst. It consists of those at the bottom but also at the edges of our society, where there are no firms to provide 'employment', and where worklessness is only solvable by effort, support and values from within.

The early disciples, on the example of Jesus, did not put work as their first priority. Even a source of income did not come first. The kingdom and its demands came first, and usually led to the disciple leaving his work – Jesus, the fishermen, Matthew. Sometimes they could maintain the work as a secondary occupation, as did Paul with his tent making. The fishermen perhaps went off and did a spell at their skill in order to finance the mission. Always the mission came first.

Wesley, as already stated, lived on an Oxford Fellowship until 1751. Thereafter he survived as he could with bits of money from writing, and from receiving hospitality. Always the mission came first. He helped many others to get work going, not only for itself, but also to support the mission. The demand for part of the mission was the clamant need all around. He organized his members to give clothes and money. But also:

> My design is to employ, for the present, all the women who are out of business, and desire it, in knitting. To these

we will first give the common price for what they do, and then add, according as they need (*Journal*, 7 May 1741).

The new obedience for today must face the problem of worklessness with the gospel response – *share work*! If society as a whole will only provide salaries for the meritocracy and the pushing, then we must develop work between us which will provide an alternative economic base. Work-sharing, co-operatives, skill exchanges, common work, wealth-sharing, all become urgent areas for us to pursue. We must learn to be communitarian entrepreneurs!

4. The new obedience – 2

The last three areas of our new obedience move us much more from corporate to personal life.

4. *Isolation.* Our society has an as yet unfaced problem of loneliness, isolation and alienation. Some people are marginalized by their difference from the norm, such as blacks and gays. Others, in very large numbers, suffer the sheer and desperate isolation of living in separate, private dwellings, untouched by any possibility of sharing and community. This is especially true for the old, who make up nearly 20% of the population.

The gospel of Jesus came especially to those who were isolated from society in general. Those on the fringe of the religious, political and economic establishments were those whom Jesus sought out – the leper, the taxman, the foreigner.

Wesley recognized this condition and encouraged any changes or experiments to alleviate it. He writes in the Journal (*Works*, II, p. 415):

> I rode through one of the pleasantest parts of England to Hornby. Here the zealous landlord turned all the Methodists out of their homes. This proved a singular kindness; for they built some little houses at the end of the town, in which forty or fifty of them live together.

The new obedience for today and tomorrow is the discipline and freedom of *creating pockets of community living*, where people are accepted and included. There is a huge variety of ways of breaking down the walls we have made for the little boxes of our nuclear families; ways of living with or near each other, sharing possessions, sharing regular meals, sharing the chores, sharing childcare, and yet retaining privacy and individuality. Let Christians and Methodists pioneer, as some are doing, models such as these for others to learn from.

5. *Rootlessness*. Much has been written about the effects of the mobility of our society. The priority of work, or better work, has led to countless people moving on, moving away from family and community. Quite unable to recreate any new community, people settle for a comfortable and private life. Their roots have no soil to grow in again. All this throws the burden of finding dignity and significance back on to each individual. All have to prove themselves, find and affirm what they believe and think, create an area of life to make a mark on. The roots of place and people no longer support and sustain and feed.

Jesus felt that his contemporaries had lost their roots. Part of his radicalism was a call to return to some of the fundamentals of God's law – to go back to Israel's radical roots in the Ten Commandments, or the Jubilee. Jesus also made a community out of those who had no community. Their being together and working for the kingdom gave them deep roots of purpose and mutuality. Questions about where to live, or where to get the next meal, became, under Jesus' guidance, of very secondary importance – but also things they sorted out for themselves.

John Wesley led large numbers of rootless people in many 'societies' to grow their own new roots, to create and write their own history. The effect of the movement was to bring a new depth, new resources, new alliances into the lives of the rootless people who became the first Methodist Christians.

The new obedience thus drives contemporary Christians to *incarnation*, to choose a place to live in, a group of people to share with. And it compels them to stay there, for better for worse, growing new roots of mutual trust and reliance, new roots of understanding and gospel confidence . . . In the search for the new roots, they find themselves going back to the old roots of New Testament community and faith. The whole history of the Community Movement in the last ten to twenty years could be referred to for models.

6. *Conformism.* The final key element of our situation is that, for all our teaching of personal development, we have not taught ourselves how to resist the assumptions, pressures and ethos of society around us. We are all part of a conformist society. We assume that what experts – or friends! – say is good for us, really is good for us. We assume that if intellectuals tell us that we would be happier or more fulfilled if we were more 'liberated', then we must heed their advice. The new pressure of self-fulfillment and 'do what others do' is far more powerful for most of us than the already decayed assumptions and rules of post-Victorian Britain.

The preaching of Jesus assumes throughout that there is nothing in the assumptions of the world that does not have to be questioned. 'Whoever will preserve their life will lose it. Whoever will lose their life will save it,' simply shows that the things meant by 'life' are not to be achieved by following the crowd. When Jesus said, 'Give up all', he meant 'all' – the whole basic ethos of one's time.

Wesley saw his whole enterprise as an incredible 'act of God' in resistance to conforming to his times and their spirit.

> I cannot forbear mentioning one instance more of the goodness of God to us in the present age. He has lifted up his standard in our islands, both against luxury, profaneness and vice of every kind. Because He caused, nearly fifty years ago, as it were, a grain of mustard seed to be sown near London; and it has now grown and put forth great branches, reaching from sea to sea. Two or three poor people met together, in order to help each other to be real Christians. They increased to hundreds, to thousands, to myriads still pursuing their one point, real religion; the love of God and man ruling all their tempers, words and actions. Now I will be bold to say, such an event as this, considered in all its circumstances, has not been seen upon earth before, since the time that St. John went to Abraham's bosom (*Works*, VII, p. 166).

The new obedience for today is a *radical non-conformism.* It is not like the old non-conformism – simply because the society to which we are not to conform has changed. The contemporary assumptions regarding politics, economics, business, social relationships, sexual behaviour, honesty are all to be questioned. We need an alternative, radical consciousness, which will begin from the very basics of human existence to ask, Who are we? What is worth doing? and What can we live for?

FOUR

A Church of the People

1. *What to do?*

In the Methodist Conference of 1983, I sat in the tea-room at Middlesbrough Town Hall, and got into a heated conversation about the Conference. It was droning on and on, in its usual way. The Conference had even agreed on a Committee to look into how it could run its business better.

'Well, how would you run the Conference?' someone asked me.

'I'd run it on Wesley's lines,' I replied.

'Like a pope?' joked another.

'No, on the lines of the first Conference of 1744. The whole Conference was arranged around three subjects: (1) What to teach (2) How to teach (3) What to do.'

I think it is worth a try. It would at least mean that everyone – including the Divisions! – had to fight for their place, and to justify what they proposed, under these headings.

Normally, the question 'What to do?' is taken for granted. Things will go on as before. We must slot people and money and ideas into the existing system. And this we think is Methodism! Actually, the reverse would be Methodism – find out what you want to teach and do, and then invent structures and systems to teach and do it.

It is hard for us to believe that the church as we have it was never intended. But it is so. And every part of our system came into being not by plan but by expediency and the accident of history. In the *Plain Account of the People Called Methodists* (1745) Wesley claims that Methodists:

> had not the least expectation, at first, of any thing like what has since followed . . . no previous design or plan at all; but everything arose just as the occasion offered. They saw or felt some impending or pressing evil, or some good end necessary to be pursued. And many times they fell unawares on the very thing which secured the good, or removed the evil. At other times, they consulted on the most probable means, following only common sense and Scripture: Though they generally found, in looking back, something in Christian antiquity likewise, very nearly parallel thereto (*Works*, VIII, p. 248).

Moreover, the design of a 'church', or even a 'connexion' of preachers, or an alliance of 'societies', was accidental. Looking back, after the Conference of 1788, Wesley writes:

> One of the most important points considered at this Conference, was that of leaving the Church. The sum of a long conversation was, (1) That, in a course of fifty years, we had neither prematurely nor willing varied from it in one article either of doctrine or discipline: (2) That we were in a course of years, out of necessity, not choice, slowly and warily varied in some points of discipline, by preaching in the fields, by extemporary prayer, by employing lay preachers, by forming and regulating societies, and by holding yearly Conferences. But we did none of these things till we were convinced we could no longer omit them but at the peril of our souls (*Journal*, VII, p. 422).

So, the heritage of John Wesley and of Methodism is not to carry out this or that method or policy or system, but simply to ask, 'What do we have to do?'

Moreover, it seems to me that Wesley is perfectly correct that the way Methodism happened was the way that things always happen when they are allowed to take place out of the dynamics present in the New Testament. Wesley himself says:

> Upon reflection, I could not but observe: This is the very thing which was from the beginning of Christianity. In the earliest times, those whom God had sent forth 'preached the gospel to every creature' . . . But as soon as any of these were so convinced of the truth, as to forsake sin and seek the gospel salvation, they immediately joined them together, took an account of their names, advised them to watch over each other, and met these 'catechumens' . . . apart from the great congregation, that they might instruct, rebuke, exhort, and pray with them, and for them, according to their several necessities (*Works*, VIII, pp. 250–251).

Therefore, the first claim of Wesley upon us today is to heed the question, What must we do?' The vast array of committees, questionnaires, surveys, synods, full-time ministers, buildings, financial appeals, and the rest can replace this question by another: 'What do these things dictate that we must do?' Thus, existing systems, structures, people, expectations and vested interests become the agenda, and the decisive questions have to be slotted into existing assumed places.

But the opposite is still possible. And even the Methodist Conference in 1984 could sit down and ask 'What must we do?' And *then* deal with everything we've already got going as ways whereby the 'things needful' get done!

2. *Whom to have?*

Second to the unasked question, 'What to do?' is another unasked question, 'Whom to have?'

I mean simply that we assume that we ought to have more of the kind of people we have got – and that means that we systematically exclude all other kinds of people.

We have seen that the middle-class Wesley became a missioner alongside the poor. Whom we have in the church depends upon whom we put ourselves alongside.

In 1983, Grace and I had the chance to visit Methodism in Western Germany. We spoke in the Ruhr, at Detmold and at the Methodist Seminary at Reutlingen. We felt at home everywhere. We could have been with the Methodists in Wales, or Northern Ireland, or South Africa, or the United States, or Switzerland, or Singapore – all places where I have worshipped and spoken. The same, or very similar, hymns, style of worship, relationship between members, exists everywhere. And the people, too, are basically very similar – middle class, traders and shopkeepers, teachers, social workers, insurance agents, clerks, occasionally business people, professors and city councillors. They are the kind of people who are very conscientious, who keep society together, who oil the wheels. They are responsible about their use of time, talents and money. They are charitable, often generous, maintaining their families and homes in a modest, controlled and often outgoing style. The fellowship life of the churches, and the devotion of the ministers, supports this kind of life-style and commitment.

The same is true in the United States. Each year since 1977 I have spent several weeks as a member of the Faculty of the Theological School of Drew University in Madison, New

Jersey. Indeed, ever since I spent a year at Drew as a student in 1954–55, I have been a regular visitor to American Methodist Seminaries and Churches. During the thirty years, US Methodist membership rose from 8 million to 10 million, and settled back to the present 8,500,000. The churches themselves continued to develop in the same direction, with Methodism an established, respected, well-organized, family-style church. No radical changes – much less changes in a radical direction! – have taken place. Friends in the USA have often asked me whether the decline of the church in Britain has anything to teach them. I have replied that I do not see any reason why an organization like the US church should decline, since it obviously fulfils so well the function of providing support and fulfilment to a predictable and apparently permanent section of middle-class America.

In Britain, we have seen in our 200 years of history, a fairly significant rise and fall in terms of numbers. Beginning with the year of John Wesley's birth, the numbers of full members of Methodist Churches in Britain has shown a fairly regular rise and fall from 72,000 in 1791, rising continually in the nineteenth century: 208,412 in 1820 to 518,156 in 1850 to 653,403 in 1880, to 770,406 in 1900. In the present century, the losses of the First World War were made up, but not those of the Second. The figures moved from 841,294 in 1910 to 801,721 in 1920, back up to 841,462 in 1930, and then down from 792,192 in 1940 to 744,815 in 1950, and from 728,589 in 1960 to 617,018 in 1970 and 487,972 in 1980. The latest figure for 1983 is 450,000. Thus between 1960 and 1980 we lost one-third of our membership. If we do the same between 1980 and 2000, we shall be down to 320,000.

The indications seem to be that the decline will continue.

To keep our present membership we need to recruit a yearly 4% of our present members. Over half of our new members are over 20 years of age, and we probably do not lose as many members as churches which make more members in their early teens. Jeffrey Harris concludes his recent study of *Can British Methodism Grow Again?* with a fairly hopeful 'Yes, if . . .' He regards the changes in the growth rate of Methodism between 1800 and 1920 as 'closely related to socio-economic change' (p. 38), and pleads that we should now work to extend our membership in the socio-economic groupings we now have.

And we still have beside our 450,000 members, around 8,000 church buildings, and 3,200 ministers. At the Union of the three Methodist denominations which form the present Church, in 1932, there were 830,000 members, 14,500 church buildings and 4,300 ministers.

But all this needs to be put into perspective. *Who* are the people whom we still have in our churches and chapels?

In *A Profile of Methodism*, Jeffrey Harris reports on the current state of Methodism. As of 1980, the situation is as follows:

	Number of Churches	*Average Members*	*Proportion of Methodists*
City Centre	116	219	5.3%
Inner City	362	88	6.6%
Council Estate	331	53	3.6%
Suburban	1,672	107	37.1%
Small Town	1,159	107	25.6%
Village/Rural	4,377	24	21.8%
	8,017	av. 100	100%

There are far more small churches than large ones. Only 466 churches have over 200 members, and 1,071 have between 100 and 200 members, but 1,414 have between 50 and 100 members, and 5,066 have less than 50 members. So we must insist: the small church is the norm for Methodism. We must stop closing or amalgamating small churches.

And we must stop abandoning our surviving churches in the inner city and the council estate. Otherwise we will be a totally suburban church.

3. Whom to be with?

'Is the Methodist Church prepared, if necessary, to die in order to live?' Thus Rupert Davies ends the 1976 edition of his book *Methodism*. Rupert Davies sees four possibilities. (1) It will remain much as it is, improving its worship, organization, evangelism, and so on. (2) It will unite with the other Free Churches, or at least the United Reformed Church, which is likely if the Anglicans reject the Ten Propositions. (3) It will unite with the other Methodist Churches to form a World Methodist Church, which would be a strong unit but would cut Methodists off from their national churches. (4) It will come closer to the Church of England, after an interim period of growing together as suggested in the Ten Propositions, thus eventually creating a 'new' church, 'greater than any of its component parts, but containing the best and most lasting elements of each', 'continuing and developing Methodist worship, order and fellowship within the larger body'.

What do the options look like in 1984?

From my point of view, I think they are very different

from those we saw ten years ago, when I would have largely agreed with Rupert Davies.

My belief is that the facts of life between the denominations at present seem to suggest that we are into a period in the eighties in which church unions are not happening, small is beautiful, and people are getting on with doing what they can in their own back yards. And I think it is a good thing.

British Methodists have lived through two schemes which have both been turned down by the Church of England – even if on minority votes. The Scheme for the Reconciliation of the Methodist and Anglican Churches was rejected by the Church of England Synods in 1969; and the proposals for 'Covenanting for Unity' were rejected in 1982. Both had obtained majorities in the Methodist Conference. In fact, the Methodists got around 80% in favour, and the Anglicans around 65%, so the differences were not great. So that, for me at least, it was rather astonishing to find that the Churches' Council for Covenanting immediately threw up its hands and said 'It's all over.' Anyway, we are now left on our own, licking our wounds. The Methodists have even lost heart for having bishops.

So, then, what ought we to do? Whom do we want to be with? Let me set down the way I see it in six suggestions.

1. There seems little point in spending years of time and energy and expense in engineering the structural, administrative and financial union of denominations which at present in so many ways tend all too easily to adopt identical stances – thoroughly middle-class ones – on all issues, and which represent precisely similar social and economic interests. A 'united' church of such similar organizations and groups would be even more conservative and bloc-like than its constituent denominations.

2. Any new form of church unity will merely bring together the established denominations – mainly Anglican, Methodist, United Reformed, and possibly Baptists. But it would need to include now also the Roman Catholics, the Pentecostalists, the West Indian denominations and the House Churches. These latter are in fact the growing churches of our time! We need to start a new kind of ecumenism, bringing in everybody.

3. Where unity is relevant in local situations, appropriate forms of local unity have been and can be devised, and can be demanded even more in future. The main enemy is the vice-like grip that denominational headquarters and area officials and committees still have. A Local Ecumenical Project (LEP) at present often has to put up with more denominational oversight and top-downward decision-making than the ordinary local church. But the opposite could be the case.

4. The two decades during which the Church of England was supposedly preparing itself for union or covenanting with other churches did not manifest any preparedness on the part of that church to deal with any of its major problems. I cannot see any likelihood of enthusiasm for any future close relationships while the Church of England remains basically oligarchic, class-ridden, priest-ridden, status-conforming, male-chauvinist, and liturgically unliberated! Some of the elements suggested in this book are, of course, in contemporary Anglicanism, here and there, fortunately. But can they now grow to overcome the other factors, which have traditionally always opposed them – as they did two hundred years ago with Wesley?

5. Now that energies are no longer being diverted by endless talk and debate about unity schemes, perhaps some other

priorities can be heeded. This book lists some of them – passionate faith, rising of the poor, radical discipleship, churches of the people, theology from the bottom. Now, if unity would help *these*, then let us have unity. But the history of church unions does not suggest that they will necessarily be served. Rather, they will be ignored yet again.

6. And cannot those of us who are still outside the magic circle of episcopacy now at last produce some contrary and gospel versions of it to confound the existing models?

As I said in the Methodist Conference of 1982, bishops could be a great opportunity to have hundreds of lay people, especially women, as local 'overseers' of the church, as a separate order from the professional fulltime, mainly male, ministers. Thus we could reclaim part of the practice of sections of the early church – to appoint lay people, and women as bishops. And thus we could provide a new model of ministry, consecrating as bishops the people – largely women – who are the instinctive and natural leaders and pastors of the people of God on the streets. Hopefully we can get into it all again, in these new ways.

4. *Whom to seek out?*

Freed from the pressure to be everything to everybody, liberated from the assumption that we must 'chaplain' everyone who comes, delivered, at least in part, from our captivity to suburbia, whom then do we go for? Whom do we seek out?

First let us be clear that in the pluralistic society of today, we cannot serve everybody, or be everywhere. 'We regard all people equally, regardless of race, colour, creed or origin', we claim. But the structures of our society have placed

Europeans, whites, Christians, and those born into 'good' families at the top. 'From the many, one' (*e pluribus unum*) is the motto of the United States. Only recently has this been seen to be oppressive to those whose only hope is in emphasizing their individuality – the Indians, the blacks and the poor. John F. Kennedy rightly said that the task now is 'to make the world safe for diversity'. 'Out of the one, many' may be the necessary motto for the future.

Wesley in principle operated on the assumption that 'whosoever will may come'. But, in fact, the very openness of his work attracted those previously outside the church. As Daniel Benham describes, in his *Memoirs of James Hutton* (1856), Wesley's audiences

> were composed of every description of persons, who, without the slightest attempt at order, assembled crying, 'Hurrah' with one breath and with the next bellowing and bursting into tears on account of their sins; some poking each others ribs, and others shouting 'hallelujah'. It was a jumble of extremes of good and evil . . . Here thieves, prostitutes, fools, people of every class, several men of distinction, a few of the learned, merchants and numbers of poor people, who had never entered a place of worship, assembled in crowds and became godly (p. 42).

The societies, once formed, contained 'more of the poor than any other sort', and even the 'other sort' were often people outside the normal semi-feudal class structures of the time. Soldiers were often there. And semi-skilled workmen, in a wide variety. As A. Skevington Wood's study of Wesley the Evangelist, *The Burning Heart*, makes clear, Wesley's 'overriding concern' was that the poor and the underprivileged should hear the gospel (cf. p. 284).

One can hardly but recall the groups and individuals who were on the fringe of the religious and political life of first-century Palestine, to whom Jesus went and out of whom the 'third estate' of the earliest church was created.

Whom to go for today?

I believe that we, like Wesley and like Jesus, must look for those at the bottom and on the fringes of our society.

We already know who they are – the people who at present are obliged to survive at the parts of our society which make the 'new obediences' of the last chapter necessary and possible. They suffer from consumerism which they cannot afford. They suffer from economic inequality, in which they are at the bottom. They suffer from worklessness, because they are not needed by any employer. They are the people left isolated by the great establishments of our time. They are the helpless victims of, or perhaps the helpless protesters against, conformism. They are the rootless, because they belong to nothing and no one.

These are those, surely, for whom we were meant, and to whom we must go. The average Christian community of any kind has few of such people. Can we not become a place where we can meet their need, just as we ourselves with our 'new obediences' move alongside them?

Of all the present denominations, Methodism might be still able to do it, here and there.

I recall some comments by an old friend, Brian Todd, after the Methodists at our council estate church at Baguley Hall (we were there 1956–62) had worshipped with the local Anglicans for three months. He wrote:

> Thank you for the lovely purpose-built church, the worthwhile congregation, the singing to an organ, being

led by a choir, the colours of their vestments, the beauty of the flowers.

So, why go back? Back to our insularity, our barn-like church and tinny piano, a handful of people and a few unruly kids, our debts ever increasing and insurmountable, the difficulty of finding people to do all the jobs necessary – stewards, leaders, secretaries, teachers, cleaners. When we have found them, where are the congregation or the scholars? What is the magic of Methodism that makes us want to go back, that makes us want to reform our splinter group in Christ's church?

Brian concluded:

Why go back? People are different, their needs are different. God made them so and perhaps the Methodist Church caters for the odd balls like me. But we are one people; one Church with a common life, a common service, the friendship and fellowship we must cement and find ways of being closer together. The ways of serving and praising God are many and He is great enough to encompass us all.

I believe we all need to 'go back' from being more and more a 'church' as an established institution, comparable to other similar churches, and go back into being a church as a community serving a movement among those at the bottom and on the fringes of society – maybe the 'odd-balls' of today.

Does this mean we become again a 'sect'? I do not think the word is right. In Troeltsch's well-known distinction between church and sect, 'church' is the place of folk religion, the chaplaincy service to society as it is, the church of the people, the cult of national life, the institution providing people at large with pieces of a faith to live by. 'Sect' for Troeltsch denotes the smaller groups of those who see themselves as 'called out' from society in general, who then create a disciplined, closed membership which exists largely for its own sake. Methodism, it has often been said, began as a sect and has become a church. And if these two types are to be accepted, there is obvious truth in the statement. However, Troeltsch took no account of the denomination – which is both church and sect, and yet neither. Even more, he took no account of the 'religious community', for which the label 'sect' is almost always as inaccurate as it is derogatory.

I have used the terms 'alternative church' or 'para church' or 'mini church' to describe the communities I have in mind. It seems to me that the kind of local Christian mini-churches which I have described in *Alternative Church* are the best method of dealing with and catering for a form of church for those at the bottom and on the fringes. Since I wrote the book (1976), it has been interesting to see how the methods have begun to be employed in a few ecumenical experiments.

I am suggesting that the need today is to create Methodist-like Christian alternative communities – alongside the state churches and denominations. Perhaps I may add a table to illustrate the way in which these three types of church are all needed, because they all cater for different groups and styles.

5. *How to serve them?*

The new model of the church which I am pleading for is not, I claim, a new one – it is one found in the New Testament and in Wesley. But it will sound strange today. So let me outline in more detail a few of its characteristics.

A Church of the People

	National Church	*Denominational Church*	*Alternative Church*
Attitude to society	Compromizes, but seeks to dominate society	Compromizes, but not to dominate society	Rejects values and way of life
Attitude of society to it	Approved	Tolerated	Ostracized
Attitude to other religious groups	Intolerant	Tolerant	Intolerant
Social ethos and concern	Generally adopts stances of society	Denomination determines ideological and social stances	Members determine ideological and social stances
Membership	Obligatory	Conventional	Voluntary
Membership requirement	Conformist, ritualistic	Formal requirements	Common experience
Social classes	All-inclusive	Middle classes	Marginal, deprived
Scope	National	National or international	Neighbourhood or sectional
Leadership	Bureaucratic	Bureaucratic	Charismatic

The new church has distinctive roles to perform, I believe, as church at the bottom, as church of the people.

1. *As church at the bottom.* The term 'base community' or 'community of the base' is well known in Latin America, and occasionally on the Continent of Europe. But it is not well known in Britain.

Yet the street-corner mission-hall, Sunday School or meeting room used to be a familiar feature of urban life. And I suggested in an article on 'Basic Communities in Britain' that there is much to be learned from the history of the do-it-yourself local congregations of the poor, however much they might appear eccentric because they are not part of the normal denominational scene. The article is in *Putting Theology to Work*, edited by Derek Winter, published by the Conference for World Mission, 1980 (pp. 59–66).

We need to discover all over again how people at the bottom of society, or on its fringes, get going their own authentic and indigenous styles of church. Methodists used to know this, as the proliferation of nineteenth-century Methodist denominations suggests. We need to discover it again.

2. *As gospel concentration*. Wesley's model of the alternative Christian community holds up and facilitates a simple concentration upon the gospel and upon gospel happenings. All the stories we have told from Wesley illustrate the point.

Such a simple concentration is hard to find in denominational churches. All the paraphernalia of the 'good' church cannot produce it – the choir, the organ, the polished pews, the white paint, the new hymn books, the modern translations, the gowned ministers, the written service sheets, the air-conditioning, the new toilets, the enlightened administration, the rationalized stewardship, the visitation secretaries, the study groups, the youth fellowship, the prayer meeting, the divisional committee, the secretaries. But occasionally in and among these things, you can find it. Not by, with or under such things, but alongside and perhaps in spite of them, you can find it.

The story of any gospel breakthrough is never wildly significant in itself. But it is the expectation of it, the importance given to it, the way things are geared in response to it, that are so significant in the Wesley story. They need to be so again today.

3. *As servicing agent to a movement.* Some mini-churches, like some established churches or denominations, live to themselves. But at least in intention, they do not exist for themselves but rather as agents whereby the movement of the kingdom can be awaited, watched for, and occasionally served and assisted.

Partly, the modesty and the smallness of the alternative church's organization and structure assist it to be more open and flexible. Partly, the only reason for there to be an alternative church is that it might provide a quicker way for people to respond to urgent issues and mission opportunities, without all the burdens of the churches and denominations.

The best models to study how this might be done would be the movements of our time – CND, WDM, Oxfam, etc., or even the political parties. We need to learn again how to activate great things from limited committed groups – and all of these might help us.

4. *As intentional community.* The alternative church is free to concentrate upon itself as a 'society', a 'community'. Wesley believed that 'Christianity is essentially a social religion'. That has political and economic implications. But it also means that the little Christian community itself is a proper concern. It is the seed-bed and the resource bank of radical discipleship and national reform.

Howard Snyder has recently 'discovered' Wesley, from outside, and writes with enthusiasm on the model of what he calls *The Radical Wesley*:

> Basic to God's economy 'which he accomplished in Jesus Christ', head of the church, is the life and witness of the Christian community, the church. John Wesley was a

radical Christian precisely because radical Christianity is not a system of doctrine but the experience of the body of Christ as a community of discipleship . . . Wesley learned what radical Christians today are beginning to stress: a *really effective struggle for social justice begins with building a biblically faithful community of Christian disciples* (p. 165).

Concern for political and social witness, and radical personal discipleship, cannot often stem from a conventional, insensitive, immature and uncommitted group of individuals in a typical contemporary church. It can only come from a community which itself manifests within itself the radical political and social values it seeks in society.

Many of the contemporary communities could help us to discover how to do this. For myself, the Ashram Community has been such a learning place.

5. *As paradigm for others.* The alternative Christian community is needed not only for its own sake, but also as a sign, a model, an example, a paradigm, for the national church and the denominations. As Wesley said, his preachers were 'extraordinary messengers, raised up to provoke the ordinary ones to jealousy' (*Works*, VII, p. 277). So, also, is the task of the alternative community.

Is it possible for there to be 'Methodist' elements within a wider ecumenical scene which would see themselves as doing specific things, performing specific functions, which might be a 'paradigm' at times for the others? It could perhaps embody in miniature some things all the churches might need to learn.

Obviously, I am here speaking of Methodist societies, Methodist communities or Methodist congregations which would be part of the wider church. They do not need to be a 'denomination'. They could exist within or between denominations.

But Methodism should be the place where they get started, or sponsored.

FIVE

Theology from the Bottom

1. Theology out of the action

Where does the method we have pursued lead us in terms of theology? This is the question with which this chapter is concerned. Especially, how does the method fit in with other contemporary models of theology?

All theology, I claim, must be theology from the bottom. It must begin, not with ideas – one's own or other people's – but with happenings. The New Testament obviously does this. John Wesley's theology is a theology from the bottom, likewise. It was theology that was reflection upon what had been happening in the world of his time on the basis of the Word of God.

Wesley has often been called a 'theologian of religious experience' and he certainly was that. Many of his writings were concerned with the religious experiences that people had, or could have, or claimed to have. But the area of personal religious consciousness is not the only area in which Wesley saw God's happenings. He also saw that other happenings of the gospel or the Bible were also taking place in the areas of secular history, community formation, morals and politics.

Perhaps Wesley is best called a 'practical theologian'. But

that implies that he *merely* provided a theology for practice, and that is not quite true. Albert Outler has called him a 'folk theologian' – one who made a theology out of the lives of people.

Recently, we have spoken of 'contextual theology', and I would like to 'try on' that label. I believe that Wesley took the context as the basis of his theology, and the context included religious experience, practice, and 'folk life', but also the whole of the life of the world at the time.

I believe that the basic method being used is that of 'contextual theology'. It is the method of contextual theologians. They proceed on the basis of the following method of 'doing theology within their own context'.

1. A social, economic and historical analysis of the situation.
2. A search for biblical and historical stories and paradigms.
3. A statement of the present 'will of God' in terms of policy for the situation.
4. Practical action in mission, politics, life-style.
5. Assessment and restatement in light of the action.

This assessment and restatement (5) then leads on to a renewed, social, economic and historical analysis of the situation (1) and the process is repeated. New Bible elements are discovered (2), preliminary statements become refined (3), new mission demands are seen (4), which themselves are reviewed after they have been carried out (5).

John Wesley, in my view, was a contextual theologian. As we have seen throughout his method was – (1) to analyse the situation, (2) to search for biblical and historical examples, (3) to seek experimentally to know God's will, (4) to encourage himself and others to act experimentally, and (5) to build practical conclusions and theological restatements.

We who do our theology and mission work alongside the

poor in the cities and who seek to develop an 'urban theology', are rightly called 'contextual theologians' also. We follow the same 5-point method. (1) The poor in the city discover from the analysis that they stand at the bottom of the social, economic and structural systems. (2) From the Bible study they discover that they as the poor are always the objects of God's special concern and the agents for God's redemptive actions. (3) From even the statements of ecumenical leaders, who are otherwise far from their companions, they hear that 'the will of God' is for the full development of all persons within a 'just, participatory and sustainable society'. (Though we do not see much practical action, much less re-assessment in the light of it!) (4) The contextual methodology of theology done by the people themselves leads to a liberation 'praxis' or activity, at least within the urban mission projects themselves. (5) Theology is re-written as a result – as has happened in many cases.

2. *Theology alongside the action*

It could be objected that Wesley's mission and thus his theology were formed out of his work among the poor, but that he himself was not poor and did not belong to the poor. This is, of course, equally true of those of us today in the West who do our mission and our theology alongside the poor, although we ourselves do not belong to the poor. What is to be said about this?

The situation of Wesley or of the Western urban theologian in this regard is the same as that of all those who have become known as liberation theologians. If one considers the background, education, life-history and life-style of most of the liberation theologians, one would have to say that the very act of theologizing is a reflective process on the struggle which most of those in the struggle have neither the interest nor the orientation to perform. It would be redundant to quote instances. But I would then have to say much more. First, the will to stand alongside and learn from the poor is a conscious and significant decision by those theologians. Second, the resulting theology has to do with the actual needs and perceptions of the poor. Third, the theologians themselves modify significantly their own life-style out of their lives among the poor. These three factors are crucial. They mean that contextual theology done alongside those in oppression and seeking for their own liberation is not an inauthentic theology. In similar vein, John Wesley and the contemporary Western urban theologian, in so far as they perform their mission, live their lives, and do their theology in the same way, carry out an authentic theological vocation, even though they do not by origin belong to the poor.

Liberation theology is, therefore, performed by those who do their work among the poor, who live among them, who adopt some of their customs, who deal daily with their problems, who listen to their pleasures, tragedies and triumphs, and who commit themselves to staying with them. They exist not as the poor, but amongst and alongside the poor. It has always been the case that Christian mission among the poor has been performed by those not initially of the poor. But those who engage in it also have to adopt some critical modifications to their own existence in order to be near enough to the poor to mission there.

Liberation theology listens to what is happening among the poor, and tells it further. What is happening is usually told in stories, so that the essential and authentic new material is the stories told by largely non-literary people. Of course, not every story is significant, but only the stories of actions which in some way reflect aspects of the gospel. The assumption is that Christianity is not a set of doctrines, but a set of happenings, continuing the happenings of the gospel. Once a happening, an action, an event, a deed, has taken place, it gets talked about by witnesses, commentators, critics, and supporters. Thus, a 'story' arises.

Liberation theology utilizes the Bible in a decisive way. The criteria whereby an action or event or aspect of the situation becomes significant are biblical criteria – above all, those of the gospel events and of the kingdom of God. The stories of contemporary people's events are set beside the stories of Jesus's events and those of his early disciples. The New Testament is seen not as a source of doctrine or belief, but rather as a way of discerning the presence of gospel-style activity now. This method is clear in volumes like Ernesto Cardinal's *The Gospel in Solentiname*, and in a forthcoming book by John D. Davies and myself, *A Worker's Mark's Gospel.*

Thus, Wesley's work – and this little book also! – belong to the area of contextual theology which is done alongside the poor, alongside God's acts of liberation in history. In that sense, Wesley and ourselves are liberation theologians. Liberation theologians from the majority world debated this hotly at the 1977 and 1982 Institute of Methodist Theological Studies at Oxford. The final decision will not be unanimous! There are problems with the word 'liberation' for us in the West, because of our special context, and because we have had so much humanistic liberation at the expense of others that we probably need bondage more than liberation in many areas – as in fact I suggested in chapter 4. We are perhaps best left calling ourselves 'contextual theologians', and getting on with doing our own theology from the bottom of our own situation, and not expecting our results or slogans to be the same, however much our methodology might be.

Essentially, 'theology from the bottom' seeks to discern the action of God within particular situations, particular people, and at particular times. Our task is today to do what the Bible did, and what Wesley did – seek to discern the Spirit, to discern the signs, to find out how the Spirit is 'taking of the things of Jesus, and showing them to disciples'. For some, it will be for bondage. For others, it will be for liberation. In the end, God decides which. John Wesley's last letter to William Wilberforce, urging him to press his anti-slavery bill in Parliament, must stand over everything we have done or said or urged, even in this modest book:

> Unless God has raised you up for this very thing
> You will be worn down by the opposition of men
> and devils.
> But if God be for you,
> who can be against you?

EPILOGUE

EPILOGUE

Our Task Today

John Wesley's genius was that, two hundred years ago—

his heart went out to those outside, and he championed a movement of common preachers;

he became part of a rising of the poor, and stood beside people seeking their liberation;

he faced the ethical and social corruption of the times, and developed radical disciplines for Christians alongside it;

he went on in faith with those who were with him, and became a pioneer of alternative forms of the church;

he heard the gospel happening in new ways all round him, and created theologies out of what the Spirit was doing.

So we, too, either people from any church or none who hear the story and want to act on it, or people within Methodism who rediscover their roots and want to build on them, need to—

Open ourselves to be moved by the realities of life today, and become passionate servants of Christ to help heal them;

Find the people suffering from oppression and disadvantage, and stand beside them as they rise up to fuller humanity;

Enter into the moral and spiritual malaise of our day, and develop prophetic new life-styles and commitments over against it;

Face the cramped and cramping denominations we have become, and help create alternatives within and alongside them;

Heed the gospel being discovered in our own time, and assist Christianity to be good news for our own history.

Recent Books

Recent Books

This list includes publication details of volumes cited in the text, together with selected other titles.

Frank Baker, *John Wesley and the Church of England*, Abingdon Press, Nashville 1970

Rupert E. Davies, *Methodism*, Revd Edn Epworth Press 1976

Jeffrey Harris, *Can British Methodism Grow Again?*, Methodist Home Mission Division 1980

Jeffrey Harris, *A Profile of Methodism*, Methodist Home Mission Division 1982

Robert Moore, *Pit-Men, Preachers and Politics*, Cambridge University Press 1974

Frederick A. Norwood, *The Story of American Methodism*, Abingdon Press, Nashville 1974

Albert Outler, *Evangelism in the Wesleyan Spirit*, Tidings, Nashville 1971

Bernard Semmel, *The Methodist Revolution*, Basic Books, New York 1973 and Heinemann, London 1974

Howard A. Snyder, *The Radical Wesley, and Patterns of Church Renewal*, Inter-Varsity Press, Illinois 1980

John J. Vincent, *Christ and Methodism: Towards a New Christianity for a New Age*, Epworth Press, London and Abingdon Press, Nashville 1965

John J. Vincent, *Alternative Church*, Christian Journals, Belfast 1976

John J. Vincent, *Into the City*, Epworth Press 1982

A. Skevington Wood, *The Burning Heart – John Wesley:*

Evangelist, Paternoster Press, Exeter and Bethany Fellowship, Minneapolis 1978

Reports and Essays

Gospel from the Poor, Urban Theology Unit, Sheffield and Methodist Home Mission Division 1984
The Living God, ed. Dow Kirkpatrick, Abingdon Press, Nashville 1971
Report of the Conversations between the Church of England and the Methodist Church, SPCK and Epworth Press 1963
Sanctification and Liberation. Liberation Theologies in Light of the Wesleyan Tradition, ed. Theodore H. Runyon, SPCK, London and Abingdon Press, Nashville 1981
Two Nations: One Gospel?, Urban Theology Unit, Sheffield and Methodist Home Mission Division 1981

John Wesley's writings are quoted from the standard editions:

The Works of the Rev. John Wesley, 3rd edn, ed. Thomas Jackson; 14 vols, Wesleyan Conference Office 1872
The Journal of the Rev. John Wesley, ed. Nehemiah Curnock; 8 vols, Epworth Press 1909–16
The Letters of the Rev. John Wesley, ed. John Telford; 8 vols Epworth Press 1931
The Standard Sermons of John Wesley, ed. E. H. Sugden; 2 vols, Epworth Press 1921

Questions for Discussion

Questions for Discussion

1. Passion of the Heart

1. Is 'The Spirit being upon me' always tied to the work described in that verse?
2. How do you, personally, 'get up and go?'
3. How can you be convinced that the Spirit is upon you, or anyone else? Does 'assurance' help?

2. Rising of the Poor

1. What form do you think a rising of the poor will take in our decades?
2. Can the rich ever help the poor? How did Wesley do it?
3. How can we act with the poor? Discuss the suggestions in section 3.

3. Radical Discipleship

1. Wesley assumes that most Christians ought to have things in common. Study the biblical evidence. What do you think?
2. What experiments in life-style change have you encountered or yourself tried out?
3. Write a 'rule of life' on the basis of the six 'new obediences'.

4. A Church of the People

1. What must you do – in your local church?
2. Assuming that Methodism is so set in its ways, with the people it has, how could it be used for people unlike us?

3. How could we assist a popular early-Methodist type of alternative church to arise outside the churches today?

5. Theology from the Bottom

1. What biblical character do you identify with most? Do the five points illumine this? Try them out as a process.
2. Describe your own context, and match up one or more biblical stories. What new insights emerge?
3. Is the gospel mainly or firstly liberation for you, or bondage?